YOUNG PAUL REVERE'S BOSTON

in 1747 was one of the world's busiest seaports, a rich, important city, the bustling capitol of Massachusetts Bay Colony. Old Boston comes vividly alive in this realistic narrative based on authentic sources.

Wherever 12-year-old Paul looks something is happening. Postriders dash out of town with mail. Farmers bring in produce. Fishmongers cry their wares. Trading ships from around the world dock at the wharves. Scarlet-coated British officers seek a friendly tavern. The Hancock mansion gleams with candlelight as Bostonians move in the sedate minuet. The Reveres, in their small wood house, sup on cod, baked beans, and brown bread.

From the time the sun strikes the copper grasshopper weathervane atop Faneuil Hall until the watchman's cry "Midnight and all is well!" this book teems with sights . . . sounds . . . smells of old Boston. Old prints, engravings, and color illustrations highlight the text.

This book is one of the How They Lived series, developed to give meaning to the study of American history. Young people will find a deeper understanding and more lasting appreciation of history and geography as they see life in the past through the eyes of those who lived it.

Young Paul Revere's Boston

Young Paul Revere's Boston

BY SAM AND BERYL EPSTEIN

ILLUSTRATED BY CARY

GARRARD PUBLISHING COMPANY
CHAMPAIGN, ILLINOIS

Picture credits:

American Antiquariam Society, Worcester, Mass.: p. 35

Bettmann Archive: p. 25, 67, 68, 69, 70

Bostonian Society, Boston, Mass.: p. 3, 6, 7, 8, 9, 65, 90

Campus Martius Museum, Marietta, Ohio: p. 66

Child Life in Colonial Days by Alice Morse Earle (New York:
The Macmillan Company, 1953): p. 61

Culver Pictures: p. 1, 21, 34, 80, 87

Library of Congress: p. 84, 86

Metropolitan Museum of Art, Collection of Mrs. Lathrop Colgate Harper: p. 57

New York Public Library Picture Collection: p. 5, 19, 28, 40, 47, 83

Old Sturbridge Village, Sturbridge, Mass.: p. 30, 60

Peabody Museum of Salem, Mass.: p. 73

Public Education in the United States by Ellwood P. Cubberley
(Boston: Houghton, Mifflin Co., 1919): p. 52

Rare Book Division, New York Public Library: p. 17, 43, 50, 77, 78

I. N. Phelps Stokes Collection, New York Public Library: p. 72

The Henry Francis du Pont Winterthur Museum, Winterthur, Delaware: Endsheets

Library of Congress Catalog Card Number: 66-13279

Contents

This plan of Boston, drawn by William Burgis, was engraved in 1728. Numbers on the map identify the following places:

1. The Common
2. Beacon Hill
3. Clark's Shipyard
4. Clark's Wharf
5. Long Wharf
6. King Street
7. North Battery
8. The Neck

1. When Paul Revere Was Twelve

When Paul Revere was growing up in Boston, the city was so small that he could walk all the way around it in a few hours.

Its narrow streets were squeezed into a hilly peninsula between the Charles River and the harbor. Water surrounded it on every side except where a narrow strip of sand tied it to the mainland. That sandy strip was called The Neck. Sometimes at high tide The Neck was under water. Then Boston was an island not much larger than a good-sized farm.

But in 1747, when Paul Revere was twelve, little Boston was one of the busiest seaports in the world. Dozens of ships were always tied up at the wharves crowding its waterfront.

This bustling capital of the Massachusetts Bay Colony was then over a hundred years old. It was one of the richest and most important cities in all of England's thirteen American colonies.

The Old State House (center) stood on bustling King Street. Long Wharf is shown in the distance.

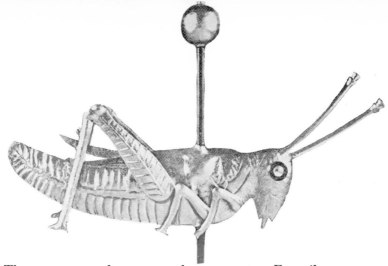

The copper grasshopper weather vane atop Faneuil
Hall still surveys Boston with its shiny glass eyes.

Boston woke up early each morning. Smoke
began to rise from hundreds of chimneys.
Housewives were stirring up the fires and
getting ready to cook breakfast. If it was
winter, they lit candles to see by. In the
summer the first rays of the sun were already
touching the city's tall church steeples and the
big weather vane on top of Faneuil Hall.

That weather vane was made in the shape
of a grasshopper. Sailors knew they were
really safe at home, at the end of a long
voyage, when they sighted the big metal insect
with its shiny glass eyes.

Every morning, when the city awoke, the
same noises were heard. Dogs barked. Chickens
cackled. Roosters crowed. Gulls screamed loudly
as they swooped overhead.

Boys whistled and shouted as they ran out to fetch water from backyard wells or a town pump. They carried it home in heavy leather or wooden buckets.

Herdsmen collected the cows that had spent the night in backyard sheds, and drove them to the big public pasture called the Common. Pigs were let out of their pens to root in the streets for their food.

The day's work was starting.

Children set off for school and workmen hurried to their· jobs. Shipbuilders in Clark's shipyard on the waterfront began to saw and hammer big timbers. Shopkeepers unlocked their doors. The tinkle of their shop bells announced the first customers of the morning.

A tailor sat down cross-legged on a big table in front of his window and began to sew buttons on a red velvet coat. A tanner started to scrape smelly cowhides in his tannery yard. Later he would soak them in big wooden vats until they were soft. Then he could sell them to shoemakers and to the makers of leather breeches and buckets and saddles.

Farmers were soon driving over The Neck into Boston through the city gate. They were delivering vegetables, fruits and meats to the

Farmers deliver food to the first-floor market of
Faneuil Hall, built by Peter Faneuil as a gift to
Boston. The second floor was used for meetings.

market on the first floor of Faneuil Hall. The
oxen pulling their wagons slipped and stumbled
on the cobblestones. The heavy wagon wheels
creaked and groaned.

The postrider passed them, trotting out of
the city with his two saddlebags full of mail.
He was heading for New York, 250 miles to
the southwest. His journey would last at least
several days.

The route he followed, called the Boston Post Road, was the oldest and most important highway in America. But it was so full of rocks and ruts and holes that nobody dared take a carriage over it. Most people did not even want to ride horseback over the road. They preferred to travel by sea. But the post-rider had to use the Post Road, so that he could deliver letters and newspapers to those who lived along his way.

Hardly had he left Boston when the fish peddlers began tooting their horns. "Fresh cod!" they called out, pushing their barrows filled with fish up one street and down another. "Fresh halibut!"

Oyster peddlers stopped before house doors and shouted, "Oys! Buy any oys?"

Every street of Boston was alive with noise and bustle. But the liveliest places of all were the city's wharves.

Boston's biggest wharf was Long Wharf. It stretched almost a third of a mile out into the harbor! A row of shops and warehouses was built along one side of it. Ships were tied up along the other side. Down the middle of the wharf, people and wagons and carts and horses came and went all day.

One Saturday morning Paul Revere's father sent him to Long Wharf on an errand. Paul's father, a silversmith, had mended a snuffbox for a sea captain. Paul was on his way to deliver the box to the captain.

Wherever Paul looked, as he walked along the wharf, something was happening. A trained dog was doing his tricks for a laughing crowd. Two dark-skinned sailors with gold rings in their ears were heading for the Green Dragon, one of Boston's many taverns.

A horse pulled a cart loaded with barrels of Boston-made rum, which were to be put aboard a ship bound for Africa.

The crew of a small fishing sloop was unloading some codfish. It had a strong smell, but the people were used to it, for codfish was one of Boston's most important products.

Three officers in scarlet uniforms sauntered down the wharf. They had come from a British man-of-war which was anchored in the harbor. Paul knew that everyone in Boston was glad to have that ship there, standing guard. She was a protection against England's enemy, France, which often made trouble for England's colonies in America.

"God bless His Majesty!" Boston men had said when the ship had arrived. "We'll drink

an extra toast to celebrate King George's birthday this year."

People smiled at the officers as they walked along. The officers smiled too. They stopped beside a ship that had docked the day before. Husky workmen, some of them Negro slaves, were unloading her cargo of raisins, wine and oranges from Spain.

"Toss us a few of those fine English oranges!" one officer shouted.

Everyone who heard him laughed. They knew that the oranges and other things in the ship's hold were smuggled goods, according to a certain English law. That law said American colonists could trade only with England or with other English colonies.

Many Boston merchants refused to obey the law. They traded with countries around the Mediterranean Sea, and they even traded with the Caribbean islands which were owned by England's enemy, France. And many English officials admitted that Boston could not remain prosperous if all its merchants obeyed that law. Even the royal governor of Massachusetts was friendly with men who dealt in smuggled goods.

So the people who laughed at the officer, when he asked for "English oranges," knew he

A merchant watches the unloading of his goods from England while his clerk keeps a careful and accurate record.

was joking. He was pretending he did not know the fruit had been smuggled. It was the kind of joke that was often made in Boston at that time.

Still smiling, the officers stopped to speak to a man whom Paul Revere recognized. Everyone else knew him too. He was a merchant named Thomas Hancock.

Thomas Hancock had started life as a poor apprentice and had become the wealthiest man in New England. People said he had proved that in the city of Boston even a poor man could make a fortune.

The small boy with Thomas Hancock was his
ten-year-old nephew, John. Some day John
Hancock would inherit his uncle's money. Then
he would spend a good deal of it helping
Americans win their freedom from England in
a revolution in which Paul Revere would also
play an important part.

But in 1747 Paul Revere could not even
imagine that such a revolution would take
place. On that particular summer day he was
probably thinking about getting home in time
for dinner. He found the sea captain who
owned the mended snuffbox and gave it to

him. Then he started back toward the Revere home on Fish Street. It was not far from the head of Clark's Wharf.

Since it was Saturday, Paul knew what his mother was cooking for dinner. Like most people in Boston, the Reveres always ate codfish on Saturday.

The custom had started more than a hundred years before, because codfish was so plentiful and cheap. Now, even people who could afford meat or chicken every day still ate codfish on Saturday. It had become a Boston custom. And Boston people thought every Boston custom was good because it was part of Boston.

They were sure that their little city, with its smells of fish and salt and tar and woodsmoke, was the finest place in all America.

2. Little Houses, Big Houses

Paul Revere's family lived in a snug wooden house built around a big chimney. There were hundreds of houses like that in the city, and some brick ones too. They stood crowded together, on the narrow sidewalks of Boston or right on the street.

Each house had its own backyard, where washing was hung to dry. People often learned news about each other from their clotheslines. "Mrs. Revere has a new baby," they said, when they saw a dozen new diapers hanging in the Reveres' backyard.

A big house might have a kitchen, a sitting room, a dining room and several bedrooms. A small house, like the Reveres', might have only a bedroom or two and a room called the keeping room. The Reveres used their keeping room as kitchen, dining room, sitting room, bedroom and bathroom too.

Mrs. Revere tried to keep a fire going all the time in her keeping room fireplace. Each evening she let the blaze burn down to a few red embers. Then she covered them with ashes. In the morning she raked the ashes away and blew on the embers until they burst into flame.

It was not easy for a housewife to prepare dinner in her fireplace. This turkey was cooked on a chain hanging over the fire instead of on a turning spit.

If the fire went out, she might hand Paul the tinderbox and tell him to start it again. In the box was a bit of dry moss or charred linen, called tinder, and pieces of steel and flint. Paul struck the steel against the flint until sparks flew into the tinder and set it aglow. Then he used the glowing tinder to light a fire.

Starting a fire by this method was a slow job, however. It could take half an hour. So Mrs. Revere sometimes sent Paul next door, to "borrow" a few embers from a neighbor's fire.

The wood-panelled walls of a keeping room were usually painted blue or green or brown. The wooden floor was often painted too. Or the floor might be covered with a thin layer of sand. Sand was a very practical floor covering. When it got dirty, a housewife swept it into the street and brought in new sand from the nearest beach.

The furniture in a keeping room was simple. There was a folding table against one wall. At mealtime it was opened up in the center of the room. Grown-ups sat around it on wooden chairs. Children sat on hard benches without backs, called forms.

There were pegs on the wall to hang clothes on because there were no closets in the house.

There was a chest for blankets, and a cupboard for plates and bowls and other such things.

A baby's cradle usually stood close to the fire. There might be a bed for the mother and father in one corner of the room. The bed was quite short, because people didn't stretch out on it. They slept sitting up, leaning against a big pile of pillows.

In a crowded house, like the Reveres', the bed had tall legs so that a low bed could be kept under it. At night that low bed was pulled out into the room for the small children to sleep in. It was called a trundle bed, or truckle bed.

The mattresses on the beds were stuffed with hard scratchy straw or lumpy corn husks. Only wealthy people could afford soft mattresses stuffed with feathers.

If Paul wanted to wash, he poured some water from a bucket into a wooden bowl. Later he emptied the bowl into the street.

A keeping room was not often used as a bathroom because some people never took baths. "Bathing is unhealthy," they said. Others thought baths should be taken only once a year or on special occasions. A young woman took a bath before her wedding, for example.

The whole family often helped prepare a bride's bath. Her brother and father carried a big wooden washtub into the house and set it beside the fire. Her mother heated water in a kettle hanging over the blaze and poured it into the tub. One young sister brought a sheet to use as a towel. Another brought a wooden box of soft jellylike homemade soap.

Wealthy people could wash in their own bedrooms, which they called chambers. Servants brought them pitchers of hot water every morning and sweet-smelling hard soap that came from England.

24

Even the Governor might visit the Hancocks in their fashionable home facing Boston Common.

The Hancocks' new stone mansion on Beacon Hill was not as big as Province House, where the Governor lived. But it was the finest house in the city. It had a view of the Common, and there were gardens and orchards all around. Thomas Hancock had a stable for his three fine horses and a coach house for his carriage.

That carriage had a special low step on it, so that Mrs. Hancock could get into it easily. She needed the step, her husband once said, because she was "a little weak in the knees." The carriage was special in other ways too. Thomas Hancock wanted it to be the most fashionable one in America, so he had ordered his "chariot," as he called it, from England.

Hancock and other well-to-do men in Boston ordered many things from Europe. They all wanted to live the way rich Englishmen lived.

They bought expensive English mirrors, fine English china, crystal chandeliers, carpets for their floors, and hand-painted paper for their walls. And they hired artists to paint portraits of themselves and their wives and children.

When a rich man like Thomas Hancock gave a party for his friends, everyone in Boston knew about it. A curious crowd often stood near his door to watch the guests arrive.

British army and navy officers, dressed in their handsome uniforms, rode up to the door. Merchants came with their wives, all dressed in their grandest clothes. Sometimes the Governor came too.

The house was full of light and color, especially on a winter night. Bright fires blazed in every fireplace. Hundreds of candles glowed and flickered. Servants moved about with trays of shining glasses. Guests played whist or other card games, or danced to the music of fiddlers scraping away on their violins.

The Puritans who had settled Boston many years earlier had believed dancing was sinful, and they would not allow it. But by the time Paul Revere and John Hancock were growing up, dancing was becoming popular, especially among the well-to-do people of the city.

An evening of dancing usually started with a minuet. Couples stepped slowly back and forth, hand in hand, in time to the music. The minuet was very stately and dignified.

On a cold night the guests soon called for livelier music. The air near a fireplace might be warm enough, but the rest of a big room could be very chilly. And people couldn't warm themselves by doing the slow steps of a minuet.

The fiddlers began to play merry jigs and quick-stepping reels. The thump of heels grew faster and louder. Candle flames leaped in the chandeliers above the dancers' heads.

The evening ended with a fine supper. When it was over, the host served hot tea and hot spiced wine to those who would have a cold journey home. Servants put heated bricks in tin foot warmers, and they placed them in each carriage. The guests said good-night, and drove off. On a dark night men with lanterns walked beside the horses to lead them.

The servants went quickly to work as soon as the guests left. They carried away the glasses and plates, knives and forks. They snuffed out candles. They shivered as the fires began to die down.

Upstairs, the host and hostess sat close beside the fire in their chamber. That fire would be kept burning all night.

A maid was preparing their bed. She shut the heavy curtains that hung around it. She filled a long-handled warming pan with hot embers and moved it back and forth between the sheets. Then her master and mistress got into bed and pulled quilts and blankets up to their chins.

During a Boston winter the outside temperature often dropped below zero. Then the temperature inside a house fell almost as low. When that happened, water froze in the Hancocks' pitcher only a few feet from their bedroom fire.

On a night like that, the only really comfortable place in Boston was a bed with warm sheets, plenty of blankets, and snug curtains to close it in.

3. Pudding Time

Guests at a wealthy man's party ate much fine food—oysters and fish, hot and cold meats, vegetables and salads and several desserts.

But even wealthy families usually ate quite simple meals. Their noon dinner was their one big meal of the day. Many people ate only bread and milk for breakfast and supper.

Dinner usually began with a dish called hasty pudding or Indian pudding. It was made by boiling Indian cornmeal in a cloth bag, in a pot of water hung over the fire. Molasses or maple sugar gave it sweetness. White sugar, which was sold in big cone-shaped loaves, was too expensive to be used in this dish.

Pudding at the beginning of a meal was so common that there was a saying about it. If a man came early to a meeting or any other event, he said, "I came in pudding time."

Poor people ate plenty of this cheap pudding because they usually had very little to eat after it. Other people ate only a bite or two, so that they would be hungry for the rest of the meal.

On Saturdays, of course, the main dish after the pudding was usually codfish. On Sundays most people followed another Boston custom and ate baked beans and brown bread.

This custom grew out of the Puritan belief that no one should work on the Sabbath. Mrs. Revere could get her baked beans ready on Saturday. She put them in a heavy covered pot called a bake kettle, with molasses and a piece of salt pork. Then she piled embers around the kettle and left it in the fireplace all night. When her family came home from church on Sunday, the beans were ready to eat.

A Boston housewife did not live like the farmers' wives who raised or made almost everything they needed. A Boston housewife was often busy helping her husband tend his

business. Besides, she could not raise much in her small backyard except a few chickens and some vegetables. She bought many things at shops, at the market and from peddlers who came to her door.

She bought bread at a bakery, for example. On Saturday she bought a brown bread made with raisins and molasses to serve with her baked beans. The rest of the week she bought rye'n Injun, a bread made with rye flour and Indian cornmeal. Only wealthy people could afford white bread made with wheat flour.

Food was often bought in open-air markets like the
one at the right. The Old Feather Store on the left
sold dusters and mattresses made of feathers.

An English gentleman who visited the Boston
market wrote to his family about it. He said
he had seen fine chickens, wild pigeons and
other birds for sale there. He thought the
salmon and other fish were "exceedingly cheap."

"They sell a fine fresh cod that will weigh
a dozen pounds or more," he wrote, ". . . for
about twopence stirling."

Shad was even cheaper than salmon or
codfish. Two shad cost one English pence, or
about two cents. One story of that time tells
about a family which was sitting down at the
table to eat a shad dinner. Just then a
neighbor knocked at the door. Quickly someone

hid the fish in the cupboard, before they let the visitor in! They did not want their neighbor to know they ate such a cheap fish.

Mrs. Revere had no cold place where she could store things to keep them fresh. So in warm weather she generally bought only enough meat for each day. If she bought more, it might spoil before it could be eaten.

Butchers had no cold storage places either. The meat they sold was often what Mrs. Revere called "high." She meant it was not really fresh and it had a strong taste. She usually cooked the "high" meat in a stew called a

Boston housewives learned how to cook hare and fowl from early cookbooks such as this one.

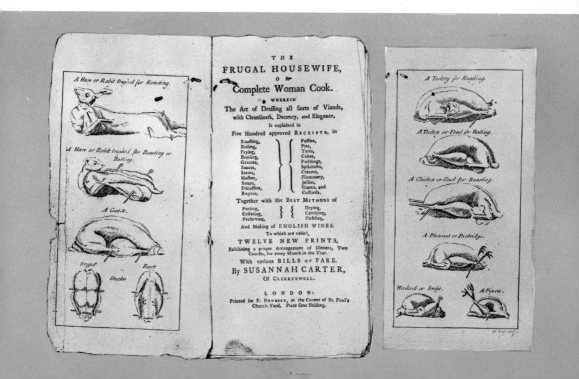

hotchpotch. She made the hotchpotch with
plenty of pepper and other spices to hide the
meat's taste.

The only way she could keep foods safely
was to dry them, preserve them or pickle them.
She might do those jobs herself, if she had
time. Or she might buy dried apples, beans
and fish, for example, and corned or pickled
meat. And she might go to the Widow
Bonyot's shop for other things.

An advertisement in a Boston newspaper
called the *Gazette* said the widow sold *All sorts
of Fruits in Preserves. Jellys and Surrups. Egg
cakes, All sorts of Macaroons, Marchpane, Crisp*

Almonds. Marchpane, or marzipan, a rich candy made of ground almonds, was the only real candy Paul Revere had ever seen.

In the winter the Reveres ate fruits and vegetables that had been dried or stored in some way so they would not spoil. When spring came, their meals changed.

In May Mrs. Revere could serve the first fresh asparagus she saw in the market and fresh dandelion leaves and other greens. In June she could treat her family to fresh strawberries and peas. All during the summer and early fall she could buy many kinds of fresh fruits and vegetables.

Meat was usually cheapest in the fall. Then farmers killed many of their cattle and sheep to save feeding them over the winter.

Christmas was not a day for feasting in Boston or for giving presents either. Even Thanksgiving was not as important a holiday as it is today. But people did sometimes celebrate a Day of Thanksgiving by going to church, and then eating a fine dinner.

Probably Mrs. Revere roasted meat for that dinner on a spit. One of Paul's small brothers might have to turn the spit around and around, so that the meat would cook evenly on all sides. Or perhaps the Reveres had a spit dog, a small dog trained to run on a moving belt that operated the spit.

Mrs. Revere and her daughter Deborah had a lot to do while the meat was roasting. They peeled and sliced turnips or squash or pumpkin, and simmered them over the fire. They called a cooked vegetable a "sause."

Perhaps they made pies too. Mince and apple pies were both favorites in Boston. There were many kinds of apple pie, such as mess apple pie, buttered apple pie and puff apple pie. Other popular apple desserts were called apple mose and apple slump.

When the meat was done, the children took their places at the table. They stood with heads bowed while their father said a prayer of thanksgiving. Then Mrs. Revere served the hasty pudding, and the feast began.

4. Waistcoats, Wigs and Ruffles

A boy like Paul Revere could dress in the morning in half a minute. Usually he slept in his shirt. So, when he jumped out of bed, he was already partly dressed.

First he pulled on his underpants and his leather knee breeches. The front and back of the breeches were exactly alike, so he could turn them around every day. This kept them from wearing out quickly.

Next he put on a sleeveless jacket of leather or heavy cotton which was called a waistcoat. It had big pockets, and buttons down the front. Usually he let his waistcoat hang open.

Then he pulled on heavy knit stockings which came up to his knees and tied them in place with a bit of cord.

Finally he stepped into a pair of heavy leather shoes decorated with big plain steel buckles. The shoes were probably not very comfortable. They were both the same shape! Paul didn't have to worry about getting the right foot into the left shoe.

Then he pulled back his hair, which came almost to his shoulders. When he had tied it at the back of his neck, he was ready for the day ahead.

John Hancock, the nephew of a wealthy man, had to spend a much longer time getting dressed. First he took off his nightshirt, which he called his night-rail or bed-waistcoat. Then he put on a fine undershirt and underpants.

Over them he wore his outer shirt and breeches. The shirt had ruffles on the sleeves and more ruffles hung from the linen band he fastened around his neck.

His breeches, made of wool or heavy silk, had a waistband that buttoned in front. Fancy silver buttons or buckles held them tight just below the knee. Ribbon garters held up his stockings of fine wool or silk.

His shoes were made of soft leather and had silver buckles. For a party he usually wore extra-light shoes called pumps. A verse of the time made fun of those shoes:

> *A pair of smart pumps made up of*
> *grain'd leather,*
> *So thin he can't venture to tread on*
> *a feather.*

John Hancock's sleeveless coat, or waistcoat, was made of satin or some other expensive material. It might have tiny flowers embroidered

Wealthy Bostonians often dressed in fine clothes like these worn by Ralph Izard during the 1700's.

all over it. He wore it buttoned, except at the top. There he left it open to show his fine neck ruffles.

Over the waistcoat he wore an open coat. Its big cuffs were turned back to show the ruffles of his shirt-sleeves.

Most boys and young men who could afford to buy fine clothes were real dandies. One visiting English gentleman said that the Boston dandies wore clothes every day which were as fine as the clothes many Englishmen wore to the coronation of a king.

Every Boston dandy wanted to wear the colors that were in the fashion. He might wear a dark-brown coat, for example, with pale tan breeches and a yellow waistcoat. His heavy winter overcoat and his cocked hat might be bright blue or deep purple. Russet stockings were especially popular. So were green ones.

Muffs were also in fashion for men. They were made of bearskin or some other fur.

John Hancock had his head shaved so that he could wear a wig. Wigs were in fashion too. They might be made with curls or with pigtails and ribbon bows. They came in blond, brown, gray and white hair. A man with a white wig sometimes had white powder shaken over it every day, so it always looked clean.

Usually a man had at least two wigs. Then he could wear one while a barber washed and curled the other.

Wigs were not very comfortable. They made one's head feel hot and itchy. A man who was spending a quiet evening at home usually took his wig off and covered his bald head with a fancy silk turban or cap. He covered his head even in bed. There he wore a nightcap, sometimes with a frilly lace border.

From the time they were about five years old, boys dressed just like grown-ups. Girls did too. Before that age, boys and girls all wore long dresses with underskirts or petticoats.

If a man said, "My son is still in petticoats," he meant the boy was very young. It was an exciting day for him and for his son when the boy took off dresses and petticoats and put on his first pair of breeches.

A girl went on wearing long skirts and petticoats when she started dressing like a grown-up. The most important change for her was that she put on stays for the first time.

Stays were narrow pieces of whalebone sewed into a wide belt, or bodice. The bodice, fastened with criss-crossed laces, was like a stiff cage. A little girl often had trouble breathing inside her stays, but she was proud of them because they made her feel grown up.

Under her skirts, a girl or woman wore a metal frame, or hoop, called a farthingale. Its shape changed from time to time to follow the latest London style. The pocket-hoop farthingale was very popular. It held a woman's skirts out at the sides in big humps.

Almost every woman kept her hair covered with a little cap. When she went out, she

The Burroughs Family by Henry Dawkins.

covered the cap with a hood or a clout. A clout was like a kerchief, or scarf, tied under the chin. Paul Revere's sister and mother wore clouts. John Hancock's wealthy aunt wore elegant hoods of velvet or silk.

In the winter women wore heavy outdoor cloaks, often made of red wool. They carried muffs covered with velvet or soft feathers.

Women's everyday shoes were made of leather. Their party shoes were made of silk in light pale colors. When they went outdoors, they strapped thick wooden soles, called clogs, over their fancy shoes. Rich women had a pair of clogs to match every pair of shoes!

Many women protected their skin also, when they went outdoors. They put on long gloves to cover their hands and arms, even in warm weather. Some of them also put on masks to shield their faces from the sun and wind!

5. Thimble Pie
and Birch Rods

Every morning except Sunday, the Widow
Thomas taught school. The schoolroom was her
own sitting room. She had a dozen pupils.
One was her own son. The oldest child in her
school was eight. The youngest was five.

The children took their places on low
benches. Dame Thomas, as they called their
teacher, stood at the front of the room. They
all bowed their heads and said a prayer. Then
the day's work began.

Words of four Syllables.

Ac-com-pa-ny	Accompany
Be-ne-vo-lence	Benevolence
Ce-re-mo-ny	Ceremony
Dif-con-tent-ed	Difcontented
E-ver-laft-ing	Everlafting
Fi-de-li-ty	Fidelity
Glo-ri-fy-ing	Glorifying
Hu-mi-li-ty	Humility
In-fir-mi-ty	Infirmity.

Words of five Syllables.

Ad-mi-ra-ti-on	Admiration
Be-ne-fi-ci-al	Beneficial
Con-fo-la-ti-on	Confolation
De-cla-ra-ti-on	Declaration
Ex-hor-ta-ti-on	Exhortation
For-ni-ca-ti-on	Fornication
Ge-ne-ra-ti-on	Generation
Ha-bi-ta-ti-on	Habitation
In-vi-ta-ti-on	Invitation

A In Adam's Fall We finned all.

B Thy Life to Mend This Book Attend.

C The Cat doth play And after flay.

D A Dog will bite A Thief at night.

E An Eagles flight Is out of fight.

F The Idle Fool Is whipt at School.

T Time cuts down all Both great and fmall.

U Uriah's beauteous Wife Made David feek his Life.

W Whales in the Sea. God's Voice obey.

X Xerxes the great did die, And fo muft you & I.

Y Youth forward flips Death fooneft nips.

Z Zacheus he Did climb the Tree His Lord to fee.

Now the Child being entred in his Letters and Spelling, let him learn thefe and fuch like Sentences by Heart, whereby he will be both inftructed in his Duty, and encouraged in his Learning.

The Dutiful Child's Promifes,

I Will fear GOD, and honour the KING.
   I will honour my Father & Mother.
I will Obey my Superiours.
I will Submit to my Elders.
I will Love my Friends.
I will hate no Man.
I will forgive my Enemies, and pray to God for them.
I will as much as in me lies keep all God's Holy Commandments.

Pages from The New England Primer.

First Dame Thomas told the pupils who were seven and eight years old to open their books. Each boy and girl owned a *New England Primer*. There were many prayers in the book and verses which told children to be good.

"Today you will learn this prayer," Dame Thomas said. She showed the oldest pupils the page where the prayer was printed.

Then Dame Thomas told the six-year-old pupils to turn to a page in their *Primers* which showed the letters of the alphabet. A little verse was printed beside each letter. She told them to learn the one for the letter *Z*. It was about a man who wanted to see Jesus Christ. It said:

> *Zaccheus he*
> *Did climb a tree*
> *His Lord to see.*

Next Dame Thomas turned to the five-year-olds. They were still learning the alphabet from a board that hung on the wall.

With a long knitting needle she pointed to the letters, one at a time. The children tried to name each letter. One small girl whispered to the girl sitting beside her.

Dame Thomas held up the finger on which she wore a silver thimble. "I shall have to give you thimble pie for whispering!" she said. She rapped the little girl on the head with the hard thimble.

Soon it was time for the oldest children to recite the prayer they had been studying. One boy had not yet learned it. Dame Thomas put a tall dunce cap on his head and made him stand in a corner. The other children all laughed at him.

Children learn their lessons in the dame's crowded keeping room.

Later the teacher taught all the children a rule for good manners at the dinner table. All recited it. "Sing not, hum not, wriggle not."

Widow Thomas's school was called a dame school. There were many like it in Boston. Paul Revere went to one when he was small. So did most of the boys he knew and many girls too. Dame schools were the only schools in the city which boys and girls attended together.

Most children paid their teacher a few pennies a week. The town of Boston paid the fee for the children of very poor families. Those pennies helped widows like Dame Thomas buy food for their families.

Children left their dame school when they were seven or eight years old. They could usually read quite well by then, and write a little too.

Some of them went to work right away to help their families. If they were lucky, their teacher had taught them a few things that would help them.

A boy might have learned some arithmetic, for example. This made him more useful to a shopkeeper or anybody else who might wish to hire him.

Young boys often looked for work on a wharf or went to sea as soon as they were old enough. Some became chimney sweeps, and crawled about inside Boston's soot-black chimneys. A chimney sweep was always soot-black himself by the end of the day.

Sometimes a girl learned to sew in a dame school. This made it easier for her to work for a dressmaker, or to earn money making shirts or hemming sheets.

Paul Revere's sister, Deborah, probably stayed home after she left dame school. Most people thought that if a girl could read her Bible, she had all the education she needed.

They said it was her duty, from then on, to help with the younger children and learn to keep house.

Learning to keep house meant learning to wash and iron, to cook and sew and clean. A girl also learned how to scrub the family's wooden dinner plates with sand until they were clean. And she learned to polish pewter.

It was hard to make a pewter pitcher shine as brightly as a silver one. A girl who could do that usually kept everything else in the house shining clean too.

"You are pewter bright!" people said, when they meant that a girl was a good housekeeper.

Deborah Revere probably made a sampler to prove she had learned how to sew. A sampler was a small piece of linen on which a girl put neat samples of all the stitches she knew. At the top she stitched the letters of the alphabet. Under them she stitched little pictures and verses. A verse many girls put on their samplers was:

When I was young and in my Prime,
You see how well I spent my Time.

Older girls and young ladies from wealthy families sometimes went to private schools

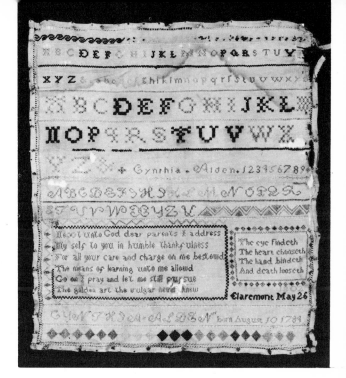

Boston girls carefully embroidered samplers like this one by thirteen-year-old Cynthia Alden.

called finishing schools. Girls came to these schools from all over New England, and even from the distant island of Jamaica. They studied music, painting and drawing. They were also taught how to behave in fashionable society. Finishing school girls learned how to dress in the latest style.

Even at school the girls wore fine clothes. One twelve-year-old pupil from Connecticut brought a dozen silk gowns with her when she came to Boston. Her teacher said twelve gowns were not enough. She told the girl's parents to buy their daughter another dress made of a rich fabric in the newest style.

Boys' schools were very different. The Puritans had planned them. In England, where they had come from, only a few well-to-do boys could get an education. The Puritans wanted every boy in Massachusetts to have the chance to go to school. Then, they thought, he would become a good Christian, a good citizen and a prosperous man. So the Puritans had built free boys' schools.

There were five of those schools in Boston in 1747. Some were called Writing Schools. They were for boys like Paul Revere who planned to learn a trade or craft. The others were called Latin Schools. They were for boys like John Hancock who hoped to go to Harvard College, which was near Boston, or perhaps to college in England.

Many people said Boston's Writing and Latin Schools were the finest public schools in the world.

Boston boys went to those schools all year long, every day except Sunday and a few holidays such as Election Day. The only money they had to pay was a small sum called "fire money." It was used to buy wood for the schoolroom fire. A poor boy did not even have to pay that.

Paul Revere went to the biggest of Boston's public schools. It was on Love Lane, in the north part of town where he lived, and was called North Writing.

Paul's teachers were men. They were usually very strict and stern. Each teacher kept a thin birch rod or stick near his desk. He used it often to punish boys who did not do their work well. A teacher usually had a leather strap too, for beating the boys.

Probably Paul went home more than once with red marks on his hands or his back.

Then, probably, his father beat him too, for being so bad that the teacher had to punish him. Most people thought a good beating was the only way to make a boy behave well and learn his lessons.

Paul learned some arithmetic and probably some grammar too. But the two most important things he studied were reading and writing.

Boys who studied in Boston's Writing Schools were able to solve problems like the one below.

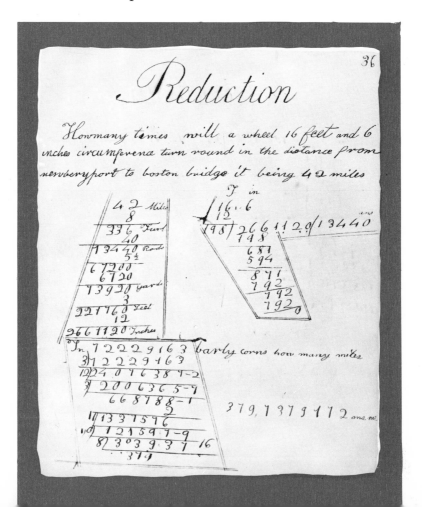

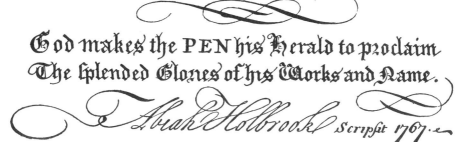

God makes the PEN his Herald to proclaim
The splended Glories of his Works and Name.
Abiah Holbrook Scripsit 1767.

Here is a sample of Master Holbrook's fancy script.

He studied reading on one floor of the two-story wooden school. Each year he and the boys in his class read more difficult books. By the time they finished Writing School, most boys were able to read and understand the laws of England and Massachusetts.

On the other floor of the school, Paul studied writing. A good handwriting was a sign that a boy was well educated. It was also very useful because all official papers and business letters had to be written by hand. A young man could usually get a good job if he could write what was called "a good hand."

The man who taught John Hancock to write at his Latin School was Master Holbrook. He was the most famous writing teacher in Boston. Many of his pupils became famous as good writers too.

John Hancock, shown here in a portrait by Copley, signed his name to legal documents in large, bold letters.

Their elegant way of shaping letters was called the "Boston style." John Hancock used it years later, when he signed the Declaration of Independence. He was the first man to put his name on that paper. He wrote it very clearly and in letters which someone said were "large enough for King George to read without his spectacles."

Writing teachers also taught boys to begin all nouns with capital letters. They believed that a lot of capital letters made a page of writing look graceful.

Although boys had to learn to write well, they did not have to worry about their spelling.

People did not believe that there was only one right way to spell a word. Some people even spelled the same word several different ways on one page. In a letter to his son, one New England farmer first spelled the word *writing* like this: *writting*. The next time he used the word, he spelled it like this: *wrighting*.

Like everyone else in Boston, schoolboys wrote with pens made of goose quills or feathers. Teachers sharpened the points on quills for young boys. Older students were allowed to sharpen their own. They mixed a dark powder with water to make their ink.

The boys had very few printed books. Often a boy made his own book out of blank pieces of paper. First he made lines on the papers with a pointed piece of lead called a plummet. Then, on those lines, he wrote what the teacher told him. Later he sewed the papers together.

A boy who owned a printed book usually wrote his name in it in the fancy Boston style. Sometimes he wrote a verse too. One popular verse was:

Steal not this Book for if You Do
The Devil will be after You.

6. Learning and Earning

Most boys were about fifteen or sixteen years old when they left public school. Then those who had gone to one of the Latin Schools often went to Harvard College, across the Charles River in Cambridge.

That's what John Hancock did and Paul Revere's best friend, Joseph Warren.

A young man who was graduated from Harvard at the age of seventeen or eighteen was ready to begin his life's work. If he wanted to be a minister, he could usually start preaching right away in some village church.

If he wanted to take up medicine, law or business, he first became an assistant to a doctor, a lawyer or a merchant.

John Hancock, for example, became an assistant to his merchant uncle. Soon he was buying and selling goods as cleverly as Thomas Hancock did.

Joseph Warren wanted to become a doctor. He indentured himself to Doctor Lloyd. This means that he agreed to work for the doctor in return for what the doctor would teach him. He went out with the doctor on his rounds.

Harvard College in 1726.

Dr. William Glysson takes the pulse of a sick woman in this old painting by Winthrop Chandler.

He watched the doctor examine sick people and treat them. He pounded up drugs and collected herbs for the medicines the doctor made. One herb he collected was called cammomile, or chammomile. It was used in an old medicine made by this recipe:

> *Chop Chammomile & crumbs of Brown Bread smal and boyl them with White Wine Vinegar, stir it wel and spred it on a cloth and binde it to the soles of the feet as hot as you can suffer it.*

This treatment was supposed to help people who did not sleep well.

When Joseph Warren thought he had learned enough, and Doctor Lloyd agreed, the young man got his doctor's license. From then on, until he died during the Revolutionary War at the Battle of Bunker Hill, he was one of Boston's favorite doctors.

Boys like Paul Revere, who did not go to college, began to learn their trade as soon as they left public school. They became the students, or apprentices, of master craftsmen.

In prosperous Boston almost every master craftsman was very busy. Almost everyone, therefore, was willing to take on an apprentice as a helper. Usually he did not even ask for the fee that masters received in other cities.

This apprentice helps his goldsmith master. Note the scales and the foot warmer.

A carpenter apprentice.

He agreed to give a boy his training, and his food and clothes too, in return for his work.

An apprentice worked fourteen or sixteen hours a day, six days a week. At first he did only simple tasks, like sweeping the floor. But he learned more every day about the trade he wanted to follow. A bright apprentice might learn his trade in a year. But he had to serve his master as an apprentice for seven years.

Some boys were apprenticed to a family friend or relative. Paul Revere was apprenticed to his own father.

Paul learned quickly how to work in silver, gold, pewter and other metals. By the time he was 21, he was his own master. Sometimes a wealthy man brought a sack of silver coins to his shop and asked Paul to melt them down and make a platter, a cup, or a silver bowl.

Boston had no banks where people could keep their money. They thought the best and safest thing to do with it was to turn it into something they could use. Of course they wanted to own something beautiful too. That is why so many of them brought their coins to Paul Revere. The beautiful things he made out of silver made him a famous silversmith before he became a famous hero of the American Revolution.

Young Paul Revere is shaping a fine silver bowl for a wealthy customer.

At the end of a young man's apprenticeship, he became a journeyman. Then he was free to work for the master who offered him the highest wages. Or he could open a shop and become a master craftsman himself.

Some men worked for wages all their lives. Usually they were paid in fish, cloth or anything else their employer had on hand. Then the workmen traded their wages for things their families needed.

A worker who received his wages in sugar, for example, might trade one pound of it to

Merchants transacted business in counting rooms like this one. Ships pictured on the wall carried Boston goods all over the world.

a farmer for a side of bacon. Later the farmer's wife might "buy" a bonnet with the sugar her husband had received.

Usually an ambitious young man wanted to become his own boss. If he didn't inherit a shop, as Paul Revere did when his father died, he tried to save or borrow enough money to start his own shop.

Many young master craftsmen wanted to become merchants too. They imported things from foreign countries to sell, along with their own wares. Or they hired extra help and made so many things that they could export some to other countries.

A Boston furniture-maker, for example, sent some of the chairs he made to the West Indies. There he exchanged them for the molasses used in rum-making, and traded the molasses for barrels of Boston rum. Then he sent the rum to Africa and exchanged it for slaves. He sold the slaves to Virginia tobacco planters at high prices.

Most people of Boston thought slavery was a bad thing. Only a few of them had slaves of their own. But there were many merchants who did not object to making money out of the slave trade.

Merchants were the richest and in some ways the most important men in Boston. But craftsmen were important too. They manufactured most of the things the people of Boston needed. They also made many things that could be traded for sugar, cotton, lemons, silk and other products which the people of Massachusetts could not make or grow.

Boston shipbuilders were probably the most important craftsmen of all. They built the vessels that brought home the valuable catches of fish and whale oil. They built the larger ships that carried on Boston's rich trade with the rest of the world.

7. The *Sea Gull* Goes to Sea

Paul Revere always knew when a big ship was going to be launched from Clark's shipyard close to his house. A crowd of eager men, women and children began to gather near the wharf. Sometimes the Governor came, riding in a fine carriage with the ship owner and his family.

One morning, soon after Paul became an apprentice, the brig *Sea Gull* was ready for launching. She towered high in the air. Her deck rose above the second-floor windows of a nearby warehouse!

The vessel rested in a sort of giant cradle
called the stocks. The stocks themselves rested
on the ways. These were heavy timbers that
lay on the ground like railroad tracks.

The ways ran straight down into the water.
They were covered with grease so that the
stocks could slide smoothly along them. Only
big blocks of wood held the ship in place at
the head of the slanting ways.

Suddenly all the noisy hammering and
sawing in the shipyard came to a halt.

Workmen climbed up on the ways, carrying
heavy sledgehammers. They lifted the hammers

high. Then they brought them down against the wooden blocks.

Crash! Crash! The hammers struck again and again.

The blows drove the blocks off the ways. The big ship, still cradled in the stocks, began to move.

"There she goes!" From all over the ship-yard, the shout went up.

The ship started slowly down the greased ways. Then she slid faster and faster.

Splash! Great sheets of water shot high into the air. She was afloat!

Timbers from the stocks pitched and tossed in the foam all around her. Frightened gulls rose from the water and wheeled overhead. The crowd cheered.

But the excitement was not yet over. A dangerous moment had come. The ship was now drifting in the busy harbor where she might harm other ships or herself.

Husky men grabbed at the shore-end of heavy lines that trailed behind the ship. They dug in their heels and pulled with all their strength. Slowly the ship began to move back toward the wharf. Finally she was tied fast.

Another Boston ship had been safely launched and berthed.

Building the *Sea Gull* had been a job of many months. It began far inland, in New England's forests. There woodsmen chopped down the tall straight oaks that would become her timbers.

Weeks went by while the logs were floated down streams and rivers to Boston harbor, and hauled ashore at the shipyard. There workmen, called sawyers, peeled off the thick oak bark and shaped the logs into great square timbers. They also sawed many of the timbers into long flat planks.

A Sawyer.

Sawing a timber into planks was done over a pit, with a big two-man saw. The timber was set in place across the top of the pit. One sawyer stood on it. A second man stood beneath, on the floor of the pit. Each held one end of the saw.

All day long the sawyers pulled their saw up and down, up and down. As its sharp teeth cut through the hard wood, sawdust showered down on the man in the pit. It got into his nose, his mouth, his eyes. Soon he was standing in sawdust up to his knees.

Men called shipwrights joined the timbers together to make the vessel's keel. They used wooden pegs called treenails or trunnels. Next they bent and cut other timbers into the shape of the ship's many ribs. They pegged the ribs to the keel. Then they added a layer of thick planks to the ribs.

Caulkers then swarmed all over the ship. Their job was to pound tarred cotton or hemp into the cracks between the planks. If those cracks were not filled, the ship would leak.

When the caulkers were finished, the ship was ready for launching. But she was still far from being ready to set off on her first voyage.

Cabinetmaker.

Shipwright

Before she could sail, she had to be fitted out, as shipbuilders put it. That job took just about as long as it had taken to build the *Sea Gull's* hull and launch her.

A whole new group of workmen took part in fitting out the ship.

Riggers carefully set her tall masts and installed her rigging.

Sailmakers sewed her thick canvas sails.

Cabinetmakers made the cupboards and bunks to be placed in the captain's cabin and the crew's quarters.

Joiners put in door and window frames, and built tables for her galley.

Painters gave her a coat of smooth gray paint and lettered *Sea Gull* on her stern.

At the same time, in long sheds not far from the shipyard, ropemakers were at work. They walked back and forth, twisting fibers in their hands, making every kind of rope the ship needed, from light cord to heavy hawsers.

In another part of Boston, coopers were making casks and barrels for carrying the ship's fresh drinking water and other supplies.

Tinsmiths were making her lanterns. Skilled instrument-makers were making her clock, her compass and the captain's navigation instruments.

In addition to making ships' items, this blacksmith and his apprentices also shod horses.

Boston's blacksmiths made the ship's hinges and bolts, and the iron braces that gave strength to her huge rudder. They made the big capstan for hauling up the anchor and the anchor chain. They made the anchor too.

A ship's anchor was one of the biggest jobs a blacksmith ever undertook. First he needed the help of all his journeymen and apprentices to hoist the heavy chunk of iron into the forge. From then on, his apprentices were busy working the bellows that kept the fire blazing. When the iron was red hot, it was hoisted out of the forge onto the anvil. There the blacksmith began to pound it into shape.

Every time the iron cooled it had to be lifted back into the fire to be reheated. For many days the lifting and heating, lifting and pounding went on, until the anchor was finally finished.

At long last the *Sea Gull* was fitted out. All the workmen aboard her walked down her gangplank for the last time.

Then the ship's barrels were filled with water, salt beef, cornmeal and all the other supplies needed for a long voyage. A crate of live chickens was put on her deck to provide eggs for the captain's breakfast. Stevedores loaded the ship's cargo, carefully stowing boxes, bundles, and casks in her hold.

Finally the captain and the ship's crew came aboard. The captain's wife walked up the gangplank with her husband. She was going with him. She knew how to make a comfortable home in a small cabin, and she enjoyed seeing strange places.

This time the crowd that had gathered at the wharf had come to watch the *Sea Gull* set sail.

Women cried. Sailors' wives knew that they would not see their husbands for many months, and might never see them again. Every woman on the wharf had relatives or friends who had been lost at sea.

But there was excitement and cheering too. A great shout went up when the ship cast off her lines.

Slowly she began to move away from the wharf as her sails filled with wind. Those on the deck called their good-byes. Those on the shore echoed them.

The *Sea Gull* moved past the islands that guarded the harbor. Out beyond them she grew smaller and smaller against the blue of the open sea.

And then she was out of sight. The *Sea Gull* was off on her maiden voyage.

8. "Midnight and All's Well"

The sound of church bells clanging in the night woke everyone in Boston.

"Fire!" people said.

In every house men and boys jumped out of bed and pulled on their breeches. A moment later they were all running toward the blaze. Each man carried a pair of leather water buckets to the fire.

In Boston's narrow streets fire could sweep from block to block with the speed of wind.

More than once it had destroyed a large part of the city. Most new houses were made of brick, so they would not burn so easily. But Boston was still crowded with wooden buildings, and fire was still a dangerous enemy.

All able-bodied men and boys became fire-fighters at the sound of the bells. They took orders from the fire warden.

The warden ordered the first men who joined him to get out the fire engine. This was a small wagon with a wooden tank and pump on it. The pump could force water out of the tank through a nozzle.

Bucket brigades like this one helped put out fires in Boston. This fire engine is more modern than the one used when Paul Revere was a boy.

Half a dozen men grabbed the ropes and pulled the wagon to the fire. As soon as they reached the spot they took turns working the pump handle up and down. This squirted a stream of water at the flames.

At the same time others formed a bucket brigade. This was a double line of men and boys stretching to the nearest well or pond. The men in one line, called the water line, handed full buckets of water from one to the other until they reached the fire. There some water was poured into the wagon's tank, so that the fire engine could keep working. The rest was splashed on the blaze or on nearby buildings which the men were trying to save.

As soon as a bucket was empty, it was handed back along the other line, called the dry line, to be filled again. Boys too young to handle heavy buckets of water were always put in the brigade's dry line.

While this was going on, other men were running in and out of burning homes and shops. They saved everything they could carry. Tables, beds, iron pots and blankets were piled up in the streets.

When the fire was finally out, the little wagon was pulled back to its station. The men and boys in the brigade lines dropped all the buckets in one heap and went home to bed.

In the morning the fire-fighters returned. Each man looked through the heap of buckets for the two that belonged to him. He knew which ones they were because he had painted or decorated them in some special way. Then he took them home and hung them beside his door, so he could grab them quickly the next time a fire broke out.

The fire warden was one of the city officials called selectmen. All selectmen were selected or chosen at a town meeting by the voters of Boston to look after certain public affairs. The

Boston citizens take part in this angry discussion during a town meeting.

town criers were also selectmen. So were the
men of the night watch.

Night watchmen patrolled the streets from
dusk to dawn. Their job was to call out the
time and the weather, as the town criers did
during the day. They also guarded the people's
safety. If a watchman saw a man on the street
after midnight, he asked why he was out so
late. If the man had no good reason, the
watchman thought he might be a thief and
took him to jail.

Boston also had officials called tithingmen.
They were supposed to keep order in the city.

Sunday was a tithingman's busiest day. He scolded boys who ran on their way to church. He pulled the ears of boys who called out to each other in loud voices.

In church he walked up and down the aisles with a long stick. It had a knob on one end, and a bushy foxtail on the other. He used the foxtail to tickle the nose of anyone who fell asleep during the sermon, which lasted for two hours or more. He used the knob at the end of the stick to rap the head of a whispering boy or a giggling girl.

Boston also had hog reeves. They looked after the hundreds of pigs that ran loose in the streets all day. Pigs ate the bones, fish heads and other food scraps which housewives threw into the street according to the custom of the times. Pigs were the only garbage collectors the city had.

Cows were not allowed to roam the streets. The city's cowherds made sure they spent the day munching the green grass on the Common and drinking from its little pond called the Frog Pond.

Schoolboys are asking a British general to stop his
soldiers from destroying their slides.

A quarter of a century later, in 1775, British
soldiers would be camping and drilling on that
same Common. The people of Boston would
look at them as enemies. But in 1747 the only
soldiers who drilled there were Boston's own
militiamen. They trained only a few times a
year, on the days called Training Days.

On a Training Day the Governor came over
from his fine mansion to watch the drilling.
Schools were closed. Apprentices and masters
left their work. Offices and shops did no
business.

90

Led by their drummers, the militia formed
lines. Some of the men were in their everyday
clothes. Some wore uniforms of red breeches
and blue coats. They marched past the
Governor and city officials. Then they turned
and marched back again. As their officers
shouted commands, they crossed the Common,
first one way then another.

"Halt! About face! Forward march!"

The men held their heads high. They tried
to look like real soldiers. But most of them
were smiling. Training Day was a holiday.

Next the militiamen shot at targets for
prizes. The prizewinners bought mugs of cider

for their friends. Peddlers with cider and food for sale did a rushing business.

Everybody had a good time. Even the noisiest children were not scolded by the tithingmen. This was one day when boys could whoop and yell as much as they liked.

Girls stood under the big elm tree in their best dresses. Young men played ball in one corner of the field. Or, if the day was hot, they headed for the waterfront and a swim.

Finally the militia officers gave their last commands. The judges of the shooting contests awarded the last prizes. Peddlers' baskets and jugs were empty. Children were tired.

"It is time to leave," mothers said. "Come now, all of you!"

"Do as your mother tells you," fathers said.

People said it had been a wonderful day. They would talk about it for many weeks. But now it was over, and the time had come for everyone to go home.

The Hancocks and the Governor's family returned to their fine mansions. The Reveres walked back to their house on Fish Street. They were all tired.

That night the watchmen called softly on their rounds, "Twelve o'clock and all is quiet. Midnight and all's well."

Glossary

apprentice: a young man who works for a craftsman so he may learn a trade

bellows: an instrument which produces a flow of air used to increase fire heat

capstan: a heavy iron post on shipboard where ropes are wound when not in use

clout: a hood worn by a girl or woman to cover her hair

cooper: a barrel-maker

farthingale: a hoop worn under wide skirts

form: a hard bench without a back

hasty pudding: a quickly-cooked pudding made of Indian cornmeal

hog reeve: a herder of hogs

hotchpotch: a highly-seasoned stew of meat and vegetables

indenture: an agreement to work for someone in exchange for training in a trade or a profession

joiner: a carpenter, usually one who fits doors and windows

journeyman: one who has been an apprentice and now works for himself or a craftsman

keeping room: a large room used as a kitchen, bedroom and sitting room

marchpane: a candy made of ground almonds, now known as marzipan

militia: a group of citizens who drill as an army, but who fight only in an emergency

night rail: a night shirt

plummet: a pointed piece of lead which makes lines on sheets of paper

rye'n Injun: a kind of bread made of rye flour and Indian cornmeal

sampler: a decorative piece of cloth that is hand-embroidered

sause: cooked vegetables

shipwright: one who builds or repairs ships

spit: a thin, pointed rod on which meat is turned and roasted over a fire

spit dog: a small dog trained to run on a moving belt which turns a spit

stevedores: men who load and unload ships in port

stocks: the frame on which a ship rests while being built

tithingman: an official who kept law and order in Boston in colonial times

trundle or truckle bed: a low bed which is stored under another bed when not in use

ways: the timbers from which a ship slides into the water during launching

Index

A VIEW OF PART OF THE TOWN OF BOSTON IN NEW